HOUGHTON MIFFLIN HARCOURT

English Language Development Program

Practice Book
Grade 2

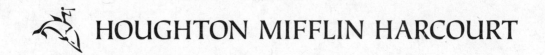

HOUGHTON MIFFLIN HARCOURT

ISBN-13   978-0-547-37238-9
ISBN-10   0-547-37238-8

4 5 6 0928 14 13 12
4500354769   ABCDEFG

Contents

High-Frequency Words

A. Look at the picture. Then write a word from the box to finish each sentence.

> until   kitchen   front

1. A good smell comes from the _____.

2. Mom cooks in _____ of me.

3. It is hard to wait _____ the food is ready!

B. Challenge Write a sentence. Use the word *kitchen*.

_____

_____

_____

Name _____

Words with Short *a, i*

A. Write a word from the box under the matching vowel sound.

sit	rat	pan
fin	bib	sad
trap	hid	cat
hand	gift	tip

Short *a* Words	Short *i* Words
1.____	2.____
3.____	4.____
5.____	6.____
7.____	8.____
9.____	10.____
11.____	12.____

B. Challenge Use words from the box to write a sentence about something you like to eat.

_____

_____

_____

Name _____

Summarize

A. Think about *Soup for Snail*. **Finish each sentence so it tells about the story.**

1. _____ is hungry.

Toad   Cat   Dog

2. Snail goes to the _____.

school   beach   store

3. Toad makes _____.

eggs   soup   pie

B. Challenge Why does Toad make the soup instead of Snail? Write a sentence that tells why.

Writing

A. Finish the sentences that describe a character from *Soup for Snail*. Use words from the word bank.

tired	good	soup
kind	goes to the store	

Toad is a _____ friend. Snail gets _____ when he

_____. This is why Toad makes Snail some _____.

Toad takes _____ care of his friend.

B. Challenge Finish the sentence.

Toad and Snail like to _____.

Vocabulary

A. Look at the pictures and the words that are under them.
   Then write a word to label each picture.

1.

an _____ sees

2.

_____ cans

3.

a _____ grows

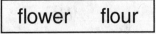

4.

wave good-_____

B. Challenge Write a sentence. Use the words *to* and *two*.

_____

_____

High-Frequency Words

A. Look at the pictures. Then write a word from the box to finish each sentence.

brought	reason	special	surprise

1. We want the birthday boy to feel

   _____.

2. We hide. Then we yell,

   "_____!"

3. Dad and I _____ a lot of

   food to the picnic.

4. We had a good _____. We

   were hungry!

B. Challenge Write a sentence. Use the word *special*.

_____

_____

_____

Name _____

Words with Short *o, u, e*

A. Write a word from the box under each picture.

> bed   hug   dog   mop

1. _____

2. _____

3. _____

4. _____

B. Challenge Use words from the box to write
a sentence about a dog.

_____

_____

_____

Summarize

A. Think about *A Surprise Pet*. Finish each sentence so it tells about the story.

1. A _____ is too big.

bird   bear   pig

2. A _____ is too tall.

giraffe   elephant   dog

3. A _____ is too wide.

bear   dog   bird

B. Challenge Which pet is just right for the girl? Write a sentence.

_____

Writing

A. Finish the sentences about *A Surprise Pet*.
Use words from the word bank. Then write another
sentence that tells why you chose your pet.

happy	makes	mess
pig	sits at the table	good
want a pig for a pet		

I don't think a _____ makes a _____ pet.

He is _____ when he _____.

He _____ a big _____. I don't

_____.

_____

_____

B. Challenge Finish the paragraph.

The best pet for me is _____. This animal will make a

great pet because _____

_____

_____

Name _____

Vocabulary

A. Write a word to label each picture.

| tall | messy | play | small |

1. a _____ *or* high building

2. a _____ *or* little mouse

3. a _____ *or* dirty pig

4. kids _____ *or* have fun

B. Challenge Finish the sentence about the boy. Use two words that have the same meaning.

The boy feels _____ or _____.

High-Frequency Words

A. Look at the pictures. Then write a word from the box to finish each sentence.

move	letter	poor	floor

1. My friend wrote me a

_____.

2. The man cleaned the

_____.

3. I _____ the box.

4. The _____ dog is lost.

B. Challenge Write a sentence. Use the word *move*.

_____

_____

_____

Name _____

Words with Long *a* and *i*

A. Write the word from the box to name the pictures.

> kite   rake   game   bike

1. _____

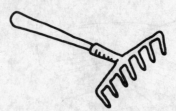

2. _____

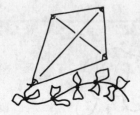

3. _____

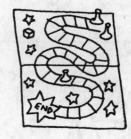

4. _____

B. Challenge Use words from the box to write about something you like to do outside.

_____

_____

_____

Name _____

Summarize

A. Think about *Lock the Gate!* **Finish each sentence so it tells about the story.**

1. Farmer Mike did not lock the _____.

gate

door

car

2. The _____ and _____ go away.

cows

pigs

sheep

B. Challenge Do you think Farmer Mike will remember to close the gate tomorrow? Write a sentence.

_____

_____

_____

Writing

A. Finish the sentences to describe a farm.
   Use words from the word bank. Then write another
   sentence that tells something else about a farm.

sweet taste	fun place to be	farm
have a picnic	want to go to the farm	green

A _____ is a _____.

We eat fruit that has a _____.

We _____ on the _____ grass.

I _____ again.

_____

_____

B. Challenge Finish the paragraph.

What place would you like to visit? I would like to go to

_____. It will be fun there because

_____

_____

Vocabulary

A. Write a word to label each picture.

soft   hard

1. a _____ rock

2. _____ grass

wet   dry

3. a _____ dog

4. a _____ dog

B. Challenge Write two sentences about two animals. Use the words *fast* and *slow*.

_____

_____

_____

Name _____

High-Frequency Words

A. Look at the pictures. Then label each picture with a word from the box.

> floor   surprise   cake   pot

1. a hot _____

2. a tile _____

3. a _____ party

4. a big _____

B. Challenge Use words from the box to write a sentence about this kitchen.

_____

_____

_____

Name _____

Fantasy and Realism

A. Look at the pictures. Circle the picture that could happen.
Draw a square around the picture that is make-believe.

B. Challenge Look at the pictures. They tell a story. We have
started the story for you. Read the beginning of the story. Then
finish writing it.

Rooster makes _____

_____

_____

Name_____

★ READERS' THEATER ★

Jack and the Beanstalk

Jack	Mother	Elda	Giant

NARRATOR: There once was a boy named Jack. One day Jack's mom told him to sell their cow. Jack did not listen to his mom. He traded the cow for five magic bean seeds.

 Mom! Look what I got! They're magic seeds.

 What did you do? Now we have no money for food!

NARRATOR: Jack's mother threw the seeds in the yard. That night the seeds grew so high that they reached the sky.

 Those seeds really were magic. The plants have grown together like a ladder!

NARRATOR: Jack climbed up the bean stalks. When he reached the clouds, he saw a castle. Standing by the door was a lady giant. Jack called up to her.

 Hello, my name is Jack. May I come in?

Directions: The teacher or a student at a higher level reads the Narrator's part. Groups of children take the other roles and read them in chorus. After several practices, the groups come together to read the whole play.

My name is Elda. Come in, but be careful. My husband eats children for breakfast.

NARRATOR: Jack soon heard a sound like thunder. The castle shook with every boom, boom, boom.

 Quick, hide in the closet! My husband is home.

 Yum, this kitchen smells like children!

 No, there are no children. You are having bean soup.

 Look at all the gold I brought home.

NARRATOR: The giant ate his meal. He counted the gold coins he had in a blue bag. Then the giant fell asleep at the table. Jack slipped out of the closet quietly.

 My mom and I could really use that gold. Careful, let's not wake him up. Got it!

NARRATOR: Jack ran to the bean plants. He climbed down. When Jack reached the ground, he saw his mother.

END PART 1

PART 2

 What is that?

 It is gold I took from a giant.

NARRATOR: Jack and his mother lived off the gold for several months. When the gold was gone, Jack visited the giant's castle again. When he arrived, he found Elda.

 Hi Elda, may I come into the castle again?

 Only until my husband comes home. Remember, he does not like children, except on toast.

NARRATOR: Soon the giant could be heard stomping through the castle. Jack hid in the closet.

 I have brought home a special hen. Watch! Lay me a golden egg.

 How clever! Now eat your bean soup.

NARRATOR: After dinner, the giant fell asleep at the kitchen table. Jack left the closet and moved silently across the kitchen floor. He put the bird in his shirt and then ran for the bean stalks. As soon as he reached them, the hen clucked loudly and woke the giant up.

Where is my hen? Who took my hen?

NARRATOR: Jack had almost reached the ground when the bean plants began to shake. The giant was climbing down the plants, too! His mom was waiting at the bottom.

 My son is back. What have you brought me?

 Take this hen and bring me the axe! We must cut down the bean plants.

 I will get you! Give me my hen!

 One, two, three, four, and five bean plants down!

 Ahhhhhhhhhhhhhhhhhhhhhh!

NARRATOR: The giant fell behind a mountain and was never heard from again. Jack took the special hen from his mother. Then he said the magic words.

 Lay me a golden egg, please.

 Wonderful! This hen is much better than our old cow!

NARRATOR: Jack, his mother, and the hen lived happily ever after.

What Is a Sentence?

A. Choose the BEST answer for each question.

1. Which group of words is a sentence?

   Ⓐ Dragons real.

   Ⓑ Dragons are not real.

   Ⓒ dragons

2. What is the naming part of this sentence?

Pig ran fast.

   Ⓐ Pig

   Ⓑ ran

   Ⓒ fast

3. What is the action part of this sentence?

Dog ate a cake.

   Ⓐ Dog

   Ⓑ ate a cake

   Ⓒ cake

B. Challenge Write a sentence about the picture. Circle the naming part of the sentence. Draw a line under the action part of the sentence.

Name _____

High-Frequency Words

A. Look at the pictures. Write a word from the box to finish each sentence.

> even   beautiful   straight   quiet

1. People are _____ in the

library. There is little noise.

2. The roof garden has _____

flowers. I love to look at them.

3. The vegetables grow in rows. Each

row is a _____ and

_____ line.

B. Challenge Write a sentence. Use the word *beautiful*. Then write a sentence using the word *straight*.

_____

_____

_____

Word with Long *o*, *u*, and *e*

A. Write a word from the box under each picture.

> bone   globe   cone
> Pete   rope   tube

1. _____

2. _____

3. _____

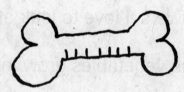

4. _____

5. _____

6. _____

B. Challenge Use words from the box to write about something you like to eat.

_____

Summarize

A. Think about *The Camping Trip*. Finish each sentence so it tells about the story.

1. First, June, Pete, and their mom and dad

_____ up a mountain slope.

draw

ski

hike

2. Next, they set up a _____.

tent

campfire

camp kitchen

3. Then, they gather water and wood to make

a _____ to cook their dinner.

tree house

chair

campfire

B. Challenge How is hiking up a hill different than hiking down a hill?

_____

Writing

A. Finish the sentences to tell your opinions about camping. Use words from the word bank. Then write another sentence that tells something else about camping.

```
        hills                      exercise
        woods                      with friends
```

I think camping is fun because it is good _____.

I like to hike up _____.

The best place to camp is in the _____.

I love to hike _____.

_____

_____

B. Challenge Finish the paragraph.

Where would you like to camp? I want to camp at

_____

_____

It will be fun to camp there because _____

_____

_____

Vocabulary

A. Write a word to label each picture.

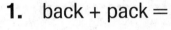

| campfire | backpack | waterfall | rainbow |

1. back + pack =

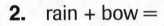

_____

2. rain + bow =

_____

3. water + fall =

_____

4. camp + fire =

_____

B. Challenge Look at the picture clues. Then put two short words together to make up one long word.

   = _____

Write four other compound words you know.

_____   _____

_____   _____

High-Frequency Words

A. Look at the picture. Then write a word from the box to finish each sentence.

important	busy	young	later

1. The city street is _____. People pass in a rush.

2. It is _____ to walk with care.

3. The _____ must learn to look before they cross the street.

4. The shops close _____ in the day.

B. Challenge Write a sentence. Use the word *important*. Then write a sentence using a different word from the box.

_____

_____

Consonant Clusters with *r*

A. Write a word from the box under each picture.

grass	crab	trash
brick	drum	frog

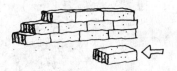

1. _____

2. _____

3. _____

4. _____

5. _____

6. _____

B. Challenge Use words from the box to write about something you see outside. _____

_____

Summarize

A. Think about *City Animals*. Finish each sentence so it tells about the story.

1. We look for wild animals in the _____.

city   country   town

2. We find birds in a _____.

house   nest   cage

3. We find _____ in a pond.

chipmunks   butterflies   fish

B. Challenge Write a sentence that has a fact about a wild animal that you have seen.

_____

Writing

A. Finish the sentences to write a summary paragraph about going to the park.

> slides   swings   having a picnic   friends
> play   playing baseball   bikes

I like to _____ when I go to the park.

There are _____ and _____ at the park.

It is fun to ride _____ with my _____!

Sometimes I watch the people _____ and

_____.

B. Challenge Finish the paragraph.

What was the most fun you have had at a park? I had a lot of fun

when _____

_____

The best part was when _____

_____

_____

Name _____

Vocabulary

A. Write a word to label each picture.

1.

I _____ my dog.   I _____ my dog.

2.

I feel _____ .   I feel _____ .

B. Challenge Are the birds opposites? Write a sentence to tell why or why not.

_____

_____

_____

High-Frequency Words

A. Look at the picture. Then complete each sentence with a word from the box.

> great   brother   across   stand

1. My big _____ and I go outside at night.

2. We _____ next to each other.

3. It is a _____ time for star watching.

4. We see a star shoot _____ the sky! I make a wish.

B. Challenge Write a sentence. Use the word *across*. Then write a sentence using a different word from the box.

_____

_____

Double Consonants

A. Write a word from the box under each picture.

cliff	dress	mitt
buzz	pocket	shell

1. _____

2. _____

3. _____

4. _____

5. _____

6. _____

B. Challenge Use words from the box to write about something

you wear. _____

_____

Name _____

Summarize

A. Think about *Splash!* **Use words from the box to complete the chart.**

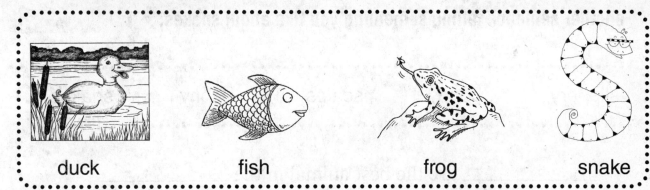

duck   fish   frog   snake

Make a list of Bill's and Nick's guesses about the animal that splashed in the pond.	
Nick's Guesses	**Bill's Guesses**
1. _____	2. _____
3. _____	4. _____

B. Challenge Write a sentence about animals you might find in the water. Then write a sentence about animals you might find in a tree.

_____

_____

_____

_____

Name _____

Writing

A. Finish the sentences to describe snakes. Use words from the word bank. You will use one word twice. Then write another sentence telling something you like about snakes.

> slippery   pond   scales   skinny   snakes

_____ are the best animal in the _____.

I like the _____ on their skin.

    It is hard to grab their _____, _____ bodies.

I really like _____.

_____

_____

B. Challenge Finish the paragraph.

    What other animals are found in ponds? In ponds there are

_____

_____

These animals are fun to watch because _____

_____

Name _____

Vocabulary

A. Write a word to label each picture. You will use each word twice.

> spring   duck

1. The _____ quacks.

_____ out of the way!

2. My favorite season

is _____.

Ow! This bed _____

pokes me!

B. Challenge Write a sentence about the bank you like best.

_____

_____

Name _____

High-Frequency Words

A. Look at the pictures. Then label each picture with a word from the box.

> smell   train   stand   straight

1. This can has a bad _____.

2. The sign says, "Go left

or _____."

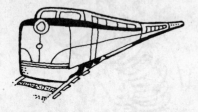

3. The _____ goes fast.

4. The people

_____ in a line.

B. Challenge Use words from the box to write a sentence about this picture of a train station.

_____

_____

_____

Fables

A. Read about fables below. Then underline the facts and circle the opinion.

Fables

A fable is a story. Fables teach a lesson about life. The characters are often animals. The animals act like people. Fables are great stories!

B. Challenge Look at the animals in the picture. Why could they be characters in a fable?

_____

_____

_____

_____

_____

_____

_____

_____

_____

43

Name _____

★ READERS' THEATER ★

The Frogs That Asked for a King

Characters			
Snap	Chumpy	Blobby	Jupiter

NARRATOR: There once were three frogs that lived in a quiet pond. Each day, they swam in the water, ate worms and bugs, and hopped up onto the land for a little sun. Nothing ever changed. Each year was like the last one.

SNAP: Ah, we live the good life. There were so many worms today. I've had my lunch and now it's time for a nap.

CHUMPY: This is not the good life. My brother who lives in the pond down the road lives the good life.

BLOBBY: What is special about your brother's pond?

CHUMPY: My brother's pond is ruled by a king!

BLOBBY: A king! Wow!

CHUMPY: We have no king. We have no leader to tell us how to spend our days.

Directions: The teacher or a student at a higher level reads the Narrator's part. Groups of children take the other roles and read them in chorus. After several practices, the groups come together to read the whole play.

© Houghton Mifflin Harcourt Publishing Company

Name _____

Cumulative Review
ELD PRACTICE BOOK

READERS' THEATER:
THE FROGS THAT ASKED
FOR A KING

SNAP: Why is that a problem?

CHUMPY: All the important ponds have kings. If I lived in an important pond, my life would be beautiful. I am going to send a message to Jupiter, the great frog god. I will ask him to send us a king.

SNAP: I wouldn't do that. Jupiter doesn't like to be bothered by us frogs.

CHUMPY: My happiness should be important to Jupiter.

BLOBBY: Your happiness is important to me, Chumpy.

CHUMPY: Thank you, Blobby. We will all feel important once we have a king.

NARRATOR: Chumpy sent his message to Jupiter by bird. The bird flew across the clouds and dropped the message in Jupiter's lap.

JUPITER: What message have you brought me, Mr. Robin? Let me read it. "Dear Jupiter, please send a king to the frogs in the south pond."

NARRATOR: Jupiter was not happy. The frogs in the south pond had plenty of water and worms and bugs. Why were they bothering him for a king?

JUPITER: Silly frogs. No king for you. You silly frogs shall get a log.

END PART 1

PART 2

NARRATOR: Jupiter tossed a large log down into the south pond. The log landed with a huge splash.

BLOBBY: What is it?

CHUMPY: Jupiter has sent us a king! Great king, the south pond frogs welcome you!

SNAP: Are all kings so quiet? Maybe we should give the king some time to fit in.

CHUMPY: Look how straight and fine this king is! He almost looks like a tree. Yes, we will give him some time.

NARRATOR: The frogs came back later. The log did not say hello. The log did not stand. The log stayed quiet.

SNAP: Can we touch him?

CHUMPY: Do not touch the king!

BLOBBY: You will make the king angry!

SNAP: I think our king is a log.

CHUMPY: A king should be strong. A king should give his frogs rules and laws.

BLOBBY: Some laws would be nice.

CHUMPY: I feel that I should send a second message to Jupiter and ask for another king.

SNAP: I wouldn't do that. Jupiter doesn't like to be bothered by us frogs.

NARRATOR: The next day Chumpy sent another message to Jupiter. Jupiter was not pleased.

JUPITER: If they want a king who will give them rules and laws, they shall have one!

NARRATOR: The king sent down a heron, a large bird that eats frogs. The large white bird flew down to the pond and rested on the log. The three frogs, who were swimming in the water, stared up at the new king.

BLOBBY: Our new king has such lovely feathers!

SNAP: Oh, no! Our new king is a heron. This bird eats frogs! Life was fine in our pond. Why couldn't you leave things as they were?

CHUMPY: I guess we can go live in my brother's pond.

NARRATOR: The three frogs left the south pond and never came back. The moral of this story is that if it isn't broken, don't fix it.

Name _____

What Kind of a Sentence?

A. Choose the BEST answer for each question.

1. What kind of sentence is this?

| Rabbit lost the race to Turtle. |

Ⓐ question

Ⓑ telling

Ⓒ command

2. Which sentence is a command?

Ⓐ You must win the race.

Ⓑ Will you please win the race?

Ⓒ I hope you win the race!

3. Which sentence is an exclamation?

Ⓐ Fables teach a life lesson.

Ⓑ Fables teach a life lesson!

Ⓒ Fables teach a life lesson?

B. Write a question about this picture. Then write the answer.

_____

_____

_____

Name _____

High-Frequency Words

A. Look at the pictures. Write a word from the box to finish each sentence.

> during   lion   winter

1. The _____ at the zoo

   roars when it is time to eat.

2. Our cat stays outside

   _____ the day. At

   night she comes inside.

3. Summer is nice, but I like

   _____ even more.

B. Challenge Write a sentence. Use the words *lion* and *winter*. Then write a sentence using a different word from the box.

_____

_____

_____

Words with *th* and *sh*

A. Write a word from the box under each picture.

fish	shark	bath
dish	thumb	three

1. _____

2. _____

3. _____

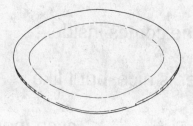

4. _____

5. _____

6. _____

B. Challenge Use words from the box to write about pet fish. _____

_____

_____

Summarize

A. Think about *Granny's Visit.* **Finish each sentence so it tells about the story.**

1. Malcolm's _____ is coming to visit.

Granny

Grandpa

friend

2. Malcolm likes Granny's _____ and _____.

treats

smile

hugs

B. Challenge **Who do you like to spend time with? What do you like to do? Finish the sentences.**

I like to spend time with _____.

We like to _____.

Writing

A. Finish the sentences to tell your opinions about eating. Use words from the word bank. You will use one word twice. Then write another sentence that tells something else about eating.

| grapes | sweet | apples |
| fruit | red | |

I like to eat _____.

The best thing about _____ is their _____ taste.

I also like to eat _____. They are _____

and juicy.

_____ are my favorite thing to eat.

_____

_____

B. Challenge Finish the paragraph.

What do you like to eat for lunch? For lunch, I like to eat

_____

_____

It is my favorite food because _____

_____

Name _____

Vocabulary

A. Write the words in ABC order.

candy	cat	cake

1. _____

treat	troop	trick

2. _____

grow	great	granny

3. _____

B. Challenge Write a sentence with the words in the box. Use the words in ABC order.

hat	hamster	happy	Hal

_____

_____

High-Frequency Words

A. Look at the picture. Write a word from the box to finish each sentence.

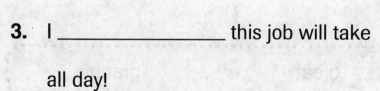

| order | guess | clothes |

1. Mom told me to put my things in

_____.

2. There are toys and _____

everywhere.

3. I _____ this job will take

all day!

B. Challenge Write a sentence. Use the words *order* and *clothes*. Then write a sentence using the word *guess*.

_____

_____

_____

_____

Vowel Pairs: *ai, ay*

A. Look at the pictures. Write a word from the box to finish each sentence.

> paint   chain   mail   tray

1. Which _____ should I

   use in my room?

2. I love getting _____.

3. That is a strong _____.

4. The girl has her lunch

   on a _____.

B. Challenge Write two sentences about art class. Use the words *paint* and *clay*.

_____

_____

_____

Name _____

Summarize

A. Think about *Ben Franklin's Fire Company*.
   Finish each sentence so it tells about the story.
   Use words from the box. You will use one word twice.

> Ben Franklin   buckets   firefighters

Ben Franklin   buckets   firefighters

1. Long ago, there were no _____.

2. People used _____ of water to put out fires.

3. _____ started a fire company.

4. Many people are saved by _____.

B. Challenge How did Ben Franklin make your life safer?

_____

_____

_____

_____

Name _____

Writing

A. Finish the sentences to tell your opinions about the fire department. Use words and phrases from the word bank. Then write another sentence that tells something else about the fire department.

> keep us safe   important
> fight fires   work for

Fire departments are _____.

Firefighters help _____.

They also _____.

I want to _____ the fire department.

_____

_____

B. Challenge Finish the paragraph.

I believe fire fighting is dangerous. Fighting fires is dangerous because

_____

_____

People who fight fires must _____

_____

Name _____

Vocabulary

A. Look at each group of pictures. Tell if the words belong at the beginning, middle, or end of the dictionary. Write B for *beginning*, M for *middle*, and E for *end*.

1. _____   kitten   firefighter

2. _____   wood   truck

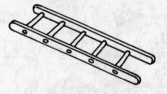 

3. _____   ladder   stairs

B. Challenge Write down three words that you would find in the beginning, middle, or end of the dictionary. After each of these words, write the letter *B, M,* or *E.* _____

_____

Name _____

High-Frequency Words

A. Look at the pictures. Write a word from the box to finish each sentence.

> behind   story   soldier

1. This is my favorite
   _____.

2. He was a _____ in
   World War I.

3. The fox is hiding _____ the
   fence.

B. Challenge Write a sentence. Use the words *story* and *soldier*. Then write a sentence using the word *behind.*

_____

_____

_____

_____

Vowel Pairs: *ow, ou*

A. Write a word from the box under each picture.

> cloud   cow   crown
> bowl   flower   house

1. _____

2. _____

3. _____

4. _____

5. _____

6. _____

B. Challenge Write a sentence to tell about the picture. Use words from the box above.

Name _____

Summarize

A. Think about *Celia and Ali*. **Finish each sentence**
so it tells about the story. Use words from the boxes.

> sick   makeup

> blouse   clothes

1. Celia was home _____.

2. She tried on Ali's _____.

3. Oh, no! Celia got _____ on Ali's shirt!

4. Ali got Celia her own _____.

B. Challenge How did Celia's mom solve the problem of the
messy shirt?

_____

_____

© Houghton Mifflin Harcourt Publishing Company

Writing

A. Finish the sentences to tell about a problem and a solution. Use words from the word bank.

> boots   rains
> umbrella   raincoat

Getting wet can be a problem when it _____.

We can wear _____.

We could also carry an _____.

I think a _____ is a great solution.

B. Challenge Finish the paragraph.

What other kind of weather can be a problem? It is a problem when

it _____

_____

_____

To fix the problem I _____

_____

_____

_____

Vocabulary

A. Read each sentence. Choose the best meaning for the underlined word. Circle the answer. Underline the word or words that helped you.

1. Sam is <u>ill</u>. He stays in bed.

sick   happy

2. Lia and Juan are <u>pals</u>. They like to play together.

enemies   friends

3. Martin is <u>bored</u>. He has nothing to do.

not interested   excited

B. Challenge Look at the picture. Read the sentence. Then write a meaning for the underlined word.

Omar is <u>pleased</u> his friends came to his party.

High-Frequency Words

A. Look at the pictures. Write a word from the box to finish each sentence.

believe	lady	whole

1. I do not _____

   in dragons.

2. Pete will eat the _____

   pizza.

3. The _____

   sews.

B. Challenge Write a sentence about the picture. Use the words *lady* and *believe*. Then write a sentence using the word *whole*.

_____

_____

_____

Vowel Pairs: *ee, ea*

A. Look at the pictures. Write a word from the box to finish each sentence.

wheel	leaf
bread	seeds

1. What kind of _____ is

this?

2. We plant _____.

3. The _____ rolled down

the hill.

4. Frog baked some

_____.

B. Challenge Write two sentences about trees. Use the words *seeds* and *leaf*.

_____

_____

_____

Summarize

A. Think about *A Week of Surprises.* **Finish each sentence so it tells about the story.**

1. Mrs. Cheng broke her _____.

2. The kids brought _____ to cheer her up.

B. Challenge Answer the questions.

3. How do the neighborhood children feel about Mrs. Cheng?

_____

4. How can you tell?

_____

Name _____

Writing

A. Write a friendly letter. Write the name of the person you are writing to. Then use words and phrases from the word bank to finish the sentences. Finally, write your name.

> play   clean   nice   project

Dear _____,

    We need your help to _____ the park.

It is important because we use the park to _____.

Another reason is to make the park look _____.

We thank you for your help with our _____.

From,

_____

B. Challenge Finish the friendly letter.

Dear _____,

    I would like to _____

Can you help me with _____

_____

_____

Vocabulary

A. Find these words in a dictionary. Draw a line to match each word with the dictionary guide words that will help you find it.

1. garden		kite – lug
2. wash		bead – bump
3. sick		cabbage – crash
4. broke		game – happy
5. listen		wag – water
6. change		sand – tea

B. Challenge Write two words that you would find on a dictionary page with the guide words *map* and *meat*.

_____

Name _____

High-Frequency Words

A. Look at the pictures. Then choose the BEST word to finish each sentence.

1.

   Jake likes to pretend he is a _____.

   Ⓐ doctor

   Ⓑ firefighter

   Ⓒ soldier

2.

   We raise _____ on our farm.

   Ⓐ cats

   Ⓑ sheep

   Ⓒ tigers

3.

   The _____ riding the horse was my favorite act.

   Ⓐ child

   Ⓑ lady

   Ⓒ man

B. Challenge Use the words *story* and *clothes* in a sentence.

_____

Topic, Main Idea, and Details

A. Read the sentences below. Circle the main idea.
   Underline the details.

Fox was a mean animal. He stole fish from
the farmer. Then he tricked Bear. He told
Bear to put his tail in the icy water for a long
time. When Bear took his tail out of the water,
his tail broke off!

B. Challenge Look at the pictures. They tell a story. We have
   started the story for you. Read the beginning of the story.
   Then finish writing it.

Bear and his friends went for a walk. They _____

_____

_____

_____

Name _____

★ READERS' THEATER ★

Why Monkeys Live in Trees

Characters				
Bush Cat	Fleas	Monkey	Snail	Elephant

NARRATOR: Our story begins with a Bush Cat that lived in the forests of Africa. Our Bush Cat was much smaller than a lion, but much larger than a house cat. This evening our Bush Cat was tired and hungry.

BUSH CAT: I am so sleepy and there was no dinner to brighten my day. The mice and squirrels were much too fast for me. Let me rest under this tree. Ouch! I hate it when the fleas bite me.

FLEAS: We bite the big, we bite the small, we do not care if you are tall.

BUSH CAT: Ouch! They bit me again. How can such tiny bugs be so troubling?

FLEAS: You may rest and think you're alone, but it's your back that we call home.

NARRATOR: At that very moment, Monkey came by. Our Monkey was smart and just a little bit tricky.

Directions: The teacher reads the Narrator's part. Groups of children take the other roles and read them in chorus. After several practices, the groups come together to read the whole play.

BUSH CAT:	Monkey, can you please pick the fleas off of my back?
MONKEY:	I guess so. Must I pick them off your whole back?
BUSH CAT:	Yes, please!
FLEAS:	For now we are gone, but we'll be back. It's you we like for our little snack.
MONKEY:	Done! Can I get a thank you? Hmmm, Bush Cat is sleeping. This is a fine time to play a joke on him.
NARRATOR:	While Bush Cat slept, Monkey tied the cat's tail to the tree. Then Monkey ran away. The next morning Bush Cat tried to get up but found that his tail had been tied to the tree.
BUSH CAT:	Who did this? The last thing that I remember was Monkey picking the fleas off of my back. He played a trick on me during the night. Help me!
SNAIL:	Be quiet! Why are you yelling so early in the morning? Most animals are still sleeping.
BUSH CAT:	I'm hungry and I'm tied to a tree. Release me!
SNAIL:	How do I know that you won't eat me once you are untied? Snails move very slowly, you know.
BUSH CAT:	I promise. You must believe me, old Snail.

END PART 1

PART 2

SNAIL: I'll help, but this may take some time. I have to inch my way down the tree first.

BUSH CAT: I'm not going anywhere.

NARRATOR Once Bush Cat was free he ran back to his cave. Then Bush Cat came up with a tricky plan of his own. He called his friends together for a meeting. At the meeting were Zebra, Elephant, Lion, and Snail. There was a great deal of noise from all the animals until Bush Cat began to speak.

BUSH CAT: Dear friends, thank you for coming. By now you have heard the whole story.

ELEPHANT: Tee hee!

BUSH CAT: Five days from now, I want you all to come to the tree where I was tied up. You must all pretend that I have died.

ELEPHANT: Should I pretend to cry?

BUSH CAT: That would be a nice touch. You might do a little dance around me as well.

NARRATOR: Five days passed, and all the animals gathered at the tree. Bush Cat lay on the ground with his eyes closed.

ELEPHANT: Boo hoo, boo hoo, I shall miss Bush Cat. We have been friends since we were babies. We would swim together at the mud hole.

FLEAS: Look who is here, oh what a sight! It's own very own supper club, and we're ready to bite.

BUSH CAT: Ouch!

SNAIL: I think we had better start dancing.

NARRATOR: The animals danced around Bush Cat in a circle. Soon after, who do you think came walking along? Monkey had come to see who was making all that noise.

MONKEY: What's going on? What happened to Bush Cat?

BUSH CAT: Nothing happened to me! I am going to tie you to this tree! You won't like it!

NARRATOR: Monkey was fast and ran up the tree. He climbed up high, where Bush Cat was unable to reach him.

BUSH CAT: Come down right now!

MONKEY: Never!

NARRATOR: This is why Monkeys live in trees. They are too scared to come down.

Name _____

Nouns

A. Choose the BEST answer for each question.

1. Read the sentence. Which word is the noun in the sentence?

> The fox was sneaky.

  Ⓐ fox

  Ⓑ was

  Ⓒ sneaky

2. Which is the correct way to spell the word that means more than one woman?

  Ⓐ womans

  Ⓑ women

  Ⓒ womens

3. Which of the following is a special noun?

  Ⓐ bear

  Ⓑ fox

  Ⓒ Farmer Brown

B. Challenge Write a sentence about the picture. Use at least two special nouns in your sentence.

_____

_____

High-Frequency Words

A. Look at the picture. Write a word from the box to finish each sentence.

> listen   told   board

1. Dan jumps off the _____

   into the water. Splash!

2. We have _____ him to

   stop many times.

3. Dan will not _____.

   He keeps jumping and splashing.

B. Challenge Write a sentence. Use the word *told*. Then write a sentence using the word *listen*.

_____

_____

_____

_____

Words with *or* and *ore*

A. Look at the pictures. Write a word from the box to finish each sentence.

fork	store	corn
torn		sword

1. I love to eat _____.

   It tastes sweet.

2. Please use your _____

   to eat your food.

3. The _____ sells food

   and drinks.

4. The paper was _____

   almost in two.

5. Tony holds his toy _____

   up high.

B. Challenge Use words from the box to write a sentence
about a day at the fair.

_____

_____

Summarize

A. Think about *Max Is a Star!* Finish each sentence so it tells about the story.

1. Max is Katie's _____. He is in a show.

cat

dog

rabbit

2. Max runs after a _____.

cat

dog

rabbit

3. Katie says he is a _____.

star

clown

winner

B. Challenge Do you think Max is a star? Explain why or why not.

_____

_____

_____

Writing

A. Finish the invitation using words and numbers from the box.

> November 9   Puppet   Classroom
> 10:30 A.M.   Mrs. Bonwin

Event _____ Show

Date _____

Time _____

Place _____

Person to contact | Call _____ at 555–1234 for more

information.

B. Challenge Write two sentences that will go on the bottom of your invitation to tell your guests what they will see at the show.

_____

_____

_____

_____

Vocabulary

A. Look at the dictionary page. Then answer the questions.

---

show • stage

S

---

show a play: *I had the part of a cat in the **show**.*

show

stage a raised stand: *The **stage** was made of wood.*

stage

---

1. How can you tell the entry words apart from the other words on the page?

   Ⓐ Entry words are in capital letters.

   Ⓑ Entry words are in darker print.

2. Which word is an entry word?

   Ⓐ part

   Ⓑ show

B. Challenge Write a dictionary entry for the word *juggle*.

_____

_____

High-Frequency Words

A. Look at the picture. Write a word from the box to finish each sentence.

> care   weigh   between

1. Jon must _____ the apple to see how heavy it is.

2. He takes great _____ not to drop the apple.

3. The apple is _____ half a pound and one pound.

B. Challenge Write a sentence. Use the word *between*. Then write a sentence using the word *care*.

_____

_____

_____

Words with *nd, nk*

A. Look at the pictures. Write a word from the box to finish each sentence.

skunk	hand	tank
think	round	wind

1. The _____ bends

   the tree.

2. Three fish swim in the

   _____.

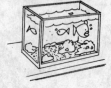

3. I hold up one finger on my

   _____.

4. The smell of _____

   was in the air.

5. The ball has a _____

   shape.

6. I like to _____ about

   answers to hard questions.

B. Challenge Use words from the box to write a sentence
about something you do or see outside.

Summarize

A. Look at the picture and think about *The Amazing Earthworm.* **Write a word from the box to finish each sentence so it tells about the story.**

waste	soil	tunnels	eat

1. Earthworms live in the

   _____ and help the

   garden grow.

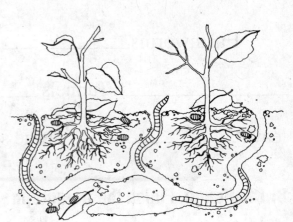

2. They _____ pieces of

   plants, fungus, and dead bugs.

3. They dig _____ in the

   soil that let in air and water. This

   helps plants to grow.

4. _____ from

   earthworms helps plants to grow.

B. Challenge How do the labels on the pictures in the *The Amazing Earthworm* help you to learn about earthworms?

_____

_____

_____

Writing

A. Finish this summary paragraph about earthworms using words and phrases from the box.

> help   becomes plant food   bring air and water
> waste   tunnels

Earthworms _____ plants. Earthworms dig

_____. Tunnels _____ to plants. Earthworms

leave _____ in the soil. The waste _____.

B. Challenge Finish the paragraph.

If I had a garden, I would _____. My plants

would grow well because _____

_____.

Vocabulary

A. Look at the pages from a thesaurus. Then answer the questions.

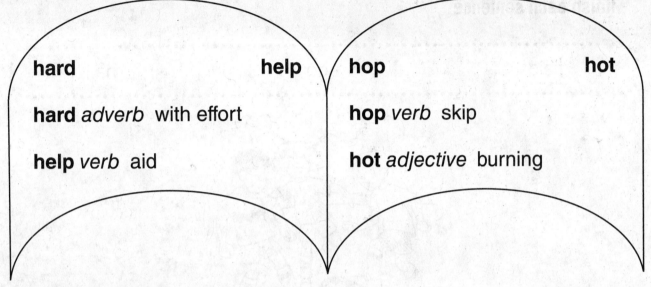

hard	**help**
hard *adverb* with effort	
help *verb* aid	

hop	**hot**
hop *verb* skip	
hot *adjective* burning	

1. Which word is a synonym for *help*?

Ⓐ aid

Ⓑ verb

Ⓒ burning

2. Read this sentence.

> The rabbit will skip across the grass.

Which is the BEST synonym for *skip*?

Ⓐ walk

Ⓑ hop

Ⓒ help

B. Challenge Write a thesaurus entry for the word *wet*.

_____

_____

High-Frequency Words

A. Look at the picture. Write a word from the box to finish each sentence.

field   ago   half

1. We kick the ball up the _____.

2. Our team started playing a long time _____.

3. Now we are in the second _____ of the game.

Go, team!

B. Challenge Write a sentence. Use the word *ago*. Then write another sentence using the word *field*.

_____

_____

_____

Name _____

Vowel Pairs *oa, ow*

A. Look at the pictures. Complete each sentence with a word from the box.

boat	snow	soap
coat	bowl	window

1. I look out my _____

    every morning.

2. _____ falls on the

    house.

3. My _____ keeps me

    warm outside.

4. _____ cleans dirt.

5. The _____ floats on the

    water.

6. We ate noodles out of a

    _____.

B. Challenge Use words from the box to write a sentence about something you do or see on a cold day.

_____

Name _____

Summarize

A. Think about *A Race to the Mountain*. Finish each sentence so it tells about the story.

1. Hummingbird and Heron race to a _____.

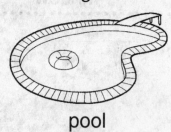
pool

field

pond

2. Hummingbird flew fast and slept during the _____.

day

night

morning

3. Heron flew slowly all _____ and all night.

day

night

morning

B. Challenge How did the way Hummingbird raced affect him?

_____

_____

_____

Writing

A. Finish this persuasive paragraph about racing, using words from the box.

> faster   school   foot   school   race   running   here

My goal is to persuade my friend to join me in a _____ race.

I have experience in _____. I want to see who is _____.

We can _____ from _____ to _____.

B. Challenge Finish the paragraph.

My goal for the summer is to _____.

_____

If you help me with this goal, then we can _____.

_____

_____

Vocabulary

A. Look at the dictionary page. Then answer the questions.

---

hare • heron

H

---

hare a fast, long-eared animal that looks like a rabbit: *I could not see the white **hare** run by in the snow.*

hare

heron a bird with a long neck, long legs, and a long bill: *The **heron** stood tall in the water.*

heron

---

1. Which of the following is a definition?

   Ⓐ a bird with a long neck, long legs, and a long bill

   Ⓑ hare

   Ⓒ *I could not see the white **hare** run by in the snow.*

2. In the entry above, *hare* is the _____.

   Ⓐ context sentence

   Ⓑ entry word

   Ⓒ definition

B. Challenge Write a dictionary entry for the word *race*. _____

_____

_____

Name _____

High-Frequency Words

A. Look at the pictures. Then label each picture with a word from the box.

```
board          half          field          between
```

1. The _____ shows the score.

2. The sandwich is cut in _____.

3. The red apple is _____ two yellow apples.

4. The girl runs down the _____.

B. Challenge Use words from the box to write a sentence about this football game.

_____

_____

_____

Poetry

A. Read about poetry below. Then draw a star next to the topic, circle the main idea, and underline the supporting details.

What Is a Limerick?

Limericks are a kind of poetry. Limericks can be funny. Limericks also use rhyme. When words rhyme, they have the same ending sounds. For example, the words *big, wig,* and *jig* rhyme. Most often, rhymes are found at the end of a line of poetry.

B. Challenge Write a funny poem about the picture. Use words that rhyme.

_____

_____

_____

Name _____

★ READERS' THEATER ★

Where to Find a Poem

| Girl | Mother | Brother | Father | Grandmother | Grandfather |

NARRATOR: There once was a girl, not long ago,
Who tried to write poetry, but it came out too slow.

GIRL: What should I write? What should I say?
If I put nothing on paper, I will be here all day!

MOTHER: Well my dear daughter, now listen to me.
It is important to write about what you can see.

BROTHER: That may be true, but for me it is what I hear.
When I play my drums, it is a poem in my ear.

FATHER: For me there is poetry in the things that I smell,
Like doughnuts and roses and a steak cooked well.

GRANDMOTHER: For me there is poetry in things that I touch,
like cat fur and velvet, hot sand, and such.

GRANDFATHER: For me there is poetry in things that I taste,
like puddings and cookies that are bad for my waist.

Directions: The teacher or a student at a higher level reads the Narrator's part. Groups of children take the other roles and read them in chorus. After several practices, the groups come together to read the whole play.

NARRATOR: The girl listened well, then she packed for a trip.

The family was traveling by car for a bit.

They were spending a week in a house in the woods,

So she brought along paper to write when she could.

GIRL: I wrote down my thoughts about things I could see.

Then I gave it to Mama who said, "Read it to me."

So here is my poem about birds in the trees.

They are tiny and brown with a small bit of white.

If you blink for a second, they dive out of sight.

BROTHER: That is nice, but what did you hear?

The sounds in the forest are all very clear.

Come with me now as I walk past that log.

You might even hear a cricket or frog.

GIRL: I went with my brother down to the lake,

We swam in the water, but make no mistake,

I listened for poems, even while wet.

Then suddenly I heard one that I'll never forget.

END PART 1

PART 2

NARRATOR: The girl swam to shore and then began to write.

She wrote all that day until it was night.

GIRL: I wrote down my thoughts about sounds in the lake,

Then I read it to my brother, who said it was great.

Here is my poem about ducks in a war.

They all quack together, but the winner honks more.

FATHER: The poem is so fine, but you did not use your nose.

Let us make supper together and see if one grows.

NARRATOR: Father gave the girl directions, as he was the cook.

They made this meal together. Then she read her book.

The stew in the pot bubbled and got warm.

The smell was so fine that a new poem was born.

GIRL: I put down my book and wrote the first line.

Then I wrote a few more and sniffed one more time.

Here, Dad, is my poem about stew in a pot.

It smells warm and so good, and I like it a lot.

GRANDMOTHER: That poem is good, but what about touch?

If you would write about that, I would like it so much.

What do you like that feels very fine,

What about a blanket that has grown soft over time?

NARRATOR: The girl felt her socks and the chair where she sat.

Then she touched the TV, but she did not like that.

GIRL: Hmm, hugs are so nice, and they are all about touch.

A poem about hugs is not asking too much.

Grandma, here is a poem that I think you will like.

One hug or two makes a perfect goodnight.

GRANDFATHER: One poem to go, you still need one more.

What about tasting all the foods in a store?

Like apples and cheeses and maybe some sweets!

You must write a poem about good things to eat!

GIRL: A poem about taste is my very last one.

This writing kept me busy, but it has also been fun.

My poem about taste is that it is always a mix.

What I like, you do not like. We have our own picks!

Possessive Nouns

A. Choose the BEST answer for each question.

1. Which word is a singular possessive noun?

The lady's perfume was smelly.

Ⓐ was

Ⓑ lady's

Ⓒ smelly

2. Which sentence has a plural possessive noun?

Ⓐ The bag's things included a tag.

Ⓑ The boy from Maine forgot his name.

Ⓒ Many boys' bags get lost on trains.

3. In which sentence is the apostrophe in the correct place?

Ⓐ Two poets' books are on sale.

Ⓑ Two poet's books are on sale.

Ⓒ Two poets books' are on sale.

B. Challenge Write a sentence about this girl from Kentucky and her ducky. Use a possessive noun.

_____

_____

_____

Name _____

High-Frequency Words

A. Write a word from the box to finish each sentence.

| middle | trouble | uncle |

1. I like spending time with my

   _____ .

2. The cat sat in the

   _____ of the map.

3. Jen did not want to get in

   _____ for breaking

   her glasses.

B. Challenge Write a sentence about the picture.
Use the word *trouble*.

_____

_____

_____

Name _____

Words with *–er* endings

A. Write the correct word next to each picture. Circle the words in which adding *–er* changed an action to a person who does the action.

> teacher   paper   dancer   flower

1. _____

2. _____

3. _____

4. _____

B. Challenge Write two sentences about teachers. Use the words *paper* and *reader*.

_____

_____

Summarize

A. Think about *Grandparents Are Fun*. **Finish each sentence so it tells about the story. Use the words in the box.**

live with   grandparents   friends

1. There are many kinds of _____.

2. Some grandparents _____ their grandchildren. Some do not.

3. Grandparents make great _____.

B. Challenge **Why do grandparents make great friends? Write a sentence.**

_____

_____

Writing

A. Finish the sentences telling an opinion of grandparents.
Use words from the word bank. Then write another sentence
that tells what grandparents do best.

> ride bikes   fun   play games
> to the park   read

Grandparents can be lots of _____.

It is fun to _____ and _____ with my grandparents.

My grandparents take me _____.

Sometimes I like it when we _____ together.

_____

_____

B. Challenge Why are grandparents good at many different
things? Finish the paragraph.

Grandparents can do many things well because _____

_____

_____ .

Name _____

Vocabulary

A. Draw a line to connect each word on the left to a word on the right that is in the same word family.

1. written   driving

2. driven   jumped

3. build   wrote

4. jump   builder

B. Challenge Write two sentences. In each sentence use a different word that is in the same word family as *teach*.

_____

_____

_____

High-Frequency Words

A. Write a word from the box to finish each sentence.

> early   instead   hair

1. Miguel got up

   _____.

2. Anna is getting her

   _____ cut.

3. Should she keep it long

   or cut it short

   _____?

B. Challenge Write two sentences about things you do in the morning. Use the words *early* and *hair*.

_____

_____

_____

_____

Name _____

Words Ending with –*le*

A. Draw a line to match each picture to the correct –*le* word.

1.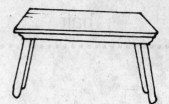

apple

2.

giggle

3.

bubble

4.

table

B. Challenge Pick two –*le* words from the box. Write a
sentence using each word.

....
....   pickle   little   puddle   middle   ....
....

_____

_____

Summarize

A. Think about *Aki's Special Gift*. **Number the sentences to put them in the correct order.**

_____ Grandfather showed Aki how to make a gift.

_____ Aki wanted to make a gift for her brother.

_____ Aki gave her gift to Yoshi.

B. Challenge List the steps that Aki followed to make a gift for her brother.

_____

_____

_____

_____

Writing

A. Finish the personal narrative. Use words from the word bank. Then add another sentence that tells about playing games with someone.

gift   I   checkers

won   player   first

My favorite birthday _____ was when I got a game called

_____. My brother and _____ spent the whole day playing

this game. The _____ time we played the game, my brother

won. The next two times we played, I _____. I am a really good

_____.

_____

_____

B. Challenge What was your favorite day that you can remember? Finish the paragraph.

My favorite day was the day when _____.

First, I _____.

Name _____

Lesson 15
ELD PRACTICE BOOK

VOCABULARY

Vocabulary

A. Read the definitions of the word *tie*. Look at the pictures.
Write the number of the definition that best matches the picture.

1. to knot the laces on a shoe

2. a contest or a game in which there is more than one winner

3. something that is worn around the neck.

_____   _____   _____

B. Challenge The word *letter* has more than one meaning.
Write two sentences with the word *letter*. Use a different
meaning in each sentence.

_____

_____

_____

_____

High-Frequency Words

A. Write a word from the box to finish each sentence.

aunt	million	pair

1. Lisa talked to her

_____ on the phone.

2. This is my favorite

_____ of mittens.

3. He has a

_____ dollars.

B. Challenge Write a sentence about what you would do if
you had a *million* dollars.

_____

_____

_____

Words with *un–*

A. Look at the pictures. Circle the word in the box that best describes each picture.

1.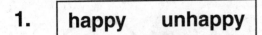
   happy   unhappy

2.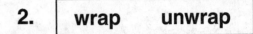
   wrap   unwrap

3. untie   tie

4. like   unlike

B. Challenge Circle the two words with the prefix *un–* in the box below. Write a sentence that uses those two words.

uncle   under   unwise   unkind

_____

_____

_____

Summarize

A. Think about *What a Birthday!* **Finish the sentences with a word from the box.**

party

brother

unhappy

1. Carla was excited about her birthday _____.

2. She was _____ when Dad said the plans had changed.

3. Then Carla got a surprise. She had a new baby _____!

B. Challenge How does Carla feel about her party being changed at the end of the story? Write a sentence.

_____

_____

_____

Name _____

Writing

A. Think about *What a Birthday!* **Finish writing a thank-you letter from Carla to her Papa. Write today's date at the top. Use words from the word bank.**

> baby brother   party   cake
> Papa   Carla

_____, 20_____

Dear _____,

Thank you for my surprise _____, my _____, and

my _____.

Love,

_____

B. Challenge Finish writing your own thank-you letter.

_____, 20 _____

Dear _____,

Thank you for _____.

_____

Love,

_____

Vocabulary

A. Look at the pictures and the words that are under them.
  Then write a word to label each picture.

1. a _____ flies

be   bee

2. a boat's _____

sail   sale

3. three _____

dear   deer

4. a juicy _____

pair   pear

B. Challenge Pick one pair of homophones above. On a separate sheet of
  paper, write two sentences. Use one homophone in each sentence.

High-Frequency Words

A. Write a word from the box to finish each sentence.

air	heavy	child	hour

1. The dad holds his

   _____.

2. He does not think the boy is

   _____.

3. The _____ was cold.

4. I will go to bed in an

   _____.

B. Challenge Write two sentences about the picture. Use the words *child*, *hour*, and *heavy*.

_____

_____

_____

_____

Words Ending with –ing

A. Look at the pictures and the words that are under them.
Then circle the correct spelling.

1. claping   clapping

2. fishing   fising

3. reading   readding

4. hoping   hopping

B. Challenge Write two sentences about something you do
at school. Use action words with the –ing ending.

_____

_____

_____

Summarize

A. Think about *A Jump in the Pool*. **Finish the sentences with a word from the box. You will use one word twice.**

afraid   jump   swim

1. Robbie knew how to _____.

2. He was _____ to jump in the water.

3. His friend Dave was _____, too.

4. Robbie showed Dave how to _____ in the water.

B. Challenge Why does Robbie jump into the pool before Dave does? Write a sentence.

_____

_____

_____

Writing

A. In *A Jump in the Pool* both Robbie and Dave were afraid to jump into the pool. Use words from the word bank to write a story paragraph about a boy who was afraid of the dark. Then write an ending to the story.

> sleep without the lights on   turn off the lights
>
> dark   I'm brave

Jin used to be afraid of the _____ .

He didn't like to _____ .

"_____," Jin said. "I will _____."

_____

_____

B. Challenge What are you afraid of? Finish the paragraph.

I am afraid of _____ . I don't _____

_____

_____

_____

_____

Vocabulary

A. Look at the words below. They all have endings that have been added to a base word. Write which base word you would look up to find these words in the dictionary.

1. running _____

2. standing _____

3. mopped _____

4. grinned _____

B. Challenge Write two sentences telling how you would find the word *shopping* in the dictionary.

_____

_____

_____

_____

Name _____

High-Frequency Words

A. Look at the pictures. Then choose the BEST word to answer each question.

1.

   Mr. Rodriguez is our _____.

   Ⓐ teacher

   Ⓑ uncle

   Ⓒ aunt

2.

   Even though it was the _____ of the night, James was still awake.

   Ⓐ early

   Ⓑ hour

   Ⓒ middle

3. Which of the following words does NOT have the prefix –*un*?

   Ⓐ unhappy

   Ⓑ unwrap

   Ⓒ uncle

B. Challenge Use the words *aunt* and *trouble* to write a sentence about the picture.

_____

_____

Cause and Effect

A. Read the sentences below. Then answer the question.

A biography is the story about a real person's life. A biography tells about causes and effects in a person's life. A cause is something that happens. Effects are the results of that event. In the biography about Dr. Davlia, his deafness was an effect. The cause was an illness.

What is an effect of Dr. Davlia going to a school for the deaf?

Ⓐ He learned to use American Sign Language.

Ⓑ He worked for the government.

Ⓒ He would give speeches.

B. Challenge Look at the picture of President George Washington. We started a biography for you. Write two more sentences for the biography.

George Washington was born on February 22, 1732. He _____

_____

_____

_____

★ READERS' THEATER ★

Clara Barton and Hurricane Katrina

Characters				
Narrator	Mrs. Tessy	Tony	Gracie	Michael

NARRATOR: Our story begins in the past. The time is September 2005. Mrs. Tessy, a teacher, is talking to her class.

MRS. TESSY: Can anyone tell me what sad and awful thing happened last week?

GRACIE: There was a big storm, a hurricane. A hurricane is a storm with strong winds and lots and lots of rain.

MRS. TESSY: You are right. The name of the storm was Hurricane Katrina. The storm caused flooding in many places in the South. Can anyone tell me what happens when there is flooding?

MICHAEL: Water goes everywhere and causes trouble. There can be water in your shoes and in your house. Sometimes there is so much water that your whole house might be under water.

Directions: The teacher or a student at a higher level reads the Narrator's part. Groups of children take the other roles and read them in chorus. After several practices, the groups come together to read the whole play.

MRS. TESSY: Hurricane Katrina left thousands of people without food and clothes and a place to sleep. I thought our class could help by having a bake sale. We will make money and then send this money to the Red Cross.

MICHAEL: What is the Red Cross?

MRS. TESSY: The Red Cross is a group that helps people. They aid people who are hurt by war and by storms like this one.

TONY: My uncle works for the Red Cross. He sometimes drives a truck to bring food to people who need it.

MRS. TESSY: This afternoon we are going to read about the lady who started the Red Cross in the United States. Her name is Clara Barton. Tomorrow I want you to report on what you have read.

MICHAEL: Is this report like a biography?

MRS. TESSY: Yes, it is!

GRACIE: Are biographies only about people from long ago?

MRS. TESSY: No, you can write a biography about someone who lives today, too. A biography is a true story about a person's life that someone has written down.

END PART 1

PART 2

NARRATOR: The next day the children gave their report on Clara Barton.

GRACIE: Clara Barton was born on December 25, 1821.

TONY: When Clara was young she was very shy. Her parents thought that maybe she needed practice talking to others. They told her to become a teacher.

MICHAEL: Clara was a teacher for more than ten years. In 1854, she moved to Washington, D.C. and stopped being a teacher.

GRACIE: There was a war in the United States that began in 1861. Clara felt that it was her duty to be sure that the soldiers had enough clothing, food, and bandages.

TONY: Clara gathered these supplies together. She asked the army if she could go where the soldiers were fighting so she could bring them these supplies.

MICHAEL: Clara did such a good job that she was put in charge of the nurses who were taking care of the soldiers.

GRACIE: When the war was over, Clara took a trip to Europe. While she was there she learned about a group that helped soldiers who were hurt or sick. This group was called the Red Cross.

TONY: Clara came back to the United States. In 1881, she helped form and lead the American Red Cross.

MICHAEL: Later, the American Red Cross chose to help all people, not just soldiers. It helps people who are hurt by things like floods and fires.

GRACIE: Clara Barton died on April 12, 1912. This weekend our class will raise money for the Red Cross. We want to help the people hurt by the hurricane.

NARRATOR: On Saturday afternoon, Mrs. Tessy's class held their bake sale. The children sold pies and cookies. On Monday morning, Mrs. Tessy told the class that they should all feel very proud.

MRS. TESSY: This past Saturday, our class raised $200 for the American Red Cross.

MICHAEL: Clara Barton would be proud of us!

Singular Possessive Nouns and the Verbs *Is/Are*

A. Choose the BEST answer for each question.

1. Which sentence is written correctly?

Ⓐ He is going to the park.

Ⓑ They is going to the park.

Ⓒ We is going to the park.

2. Which word is a singular possessive noun?

Andrew was happy that his uncle took him fishing.

Ⓐ Andrew

Ⓑ his

Ⓒ uncle

3. Which of the following is NOT a possessive noun?

Ⓐ his

Ⓑ she

Ⓒ my

B. Challenge Write two sentences about the picture. Use the verb *is* in one sentence. Use the verb *are* in one sentence.

_____

_____

High-Frequency Words

A. Look at the picture. Then complete each sentence with a word from the box.

> fair   woman   gold

1. The _____ swims under the water and looks for things.

2. She finds a _____ pot from long ago.

3. She will be _____ and show her find to others.

B. Challenge Write a sentence. Use the word *fair*. Then write another sentence and use the word *gold*.

_____

_____

_____

Words with *oo, ew, ue, ou*

A. Look at the pictures. Then complete each sentence with a word from the box.

drew	moon	soup
group	glue	broom

1. The _____ is out.

2. He _____ a picture of a girl.

3. I use _____ to stick the papers together.

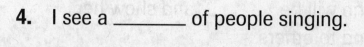

4. I see a _____ of people singing.

5. The _____ helps me clean the floor.

6. The _____ is too hot to eat.

B. Challenge Use words from the box to write two sentences about something you can make in art class.

_____

_____

_____

_____

Summarize

A. Think about *A Gift of Crayons.* Finish each sentence so it tells about the story.

1. Brooke's mom and dad bring her _____ after she has an operation.

 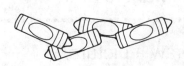 

scissors crayons flowers

2. Brooke learns that she loves to _____.

draw dance sing

3. Brooke becomes an artist and an _____teacher.

gym math art

B. Challenge Do you think the author believes that crayons help children learn to draw?

_____

_____

Writing

A. Finish the sentences to write a paragraph that explains how to draw a picture. Use words and phrases from the word bank.

> lines   want to draw   color and shade

Here is how you draw a picture.

First, you look at what you _____.

Next, you draw some _____.

Last, you _____ your picture.

B. Challenge How would you give directions for playing the game Hide and Seek? Finish the paragraph with your answer.

Here is how you play the game Hide and Seek. First, you

_____

_____

_____

_____

Name _____

Vocabulary

A. Write a base word from the box to complete the word family for each picture.

> talk   climb   kick   jump

1. _____ -ed

_____ -ing

_____ -er

2. _____ -ed

_____ -ing

_____ -er

3. _____ -ed

_____ -ing

_____ -er

4. _____ -ed

_____ -ing

_____ -er

B. Challenge Use words from the box to write a sentence about the thing you do best. Underline the base word in your sentence.

_____

_____

High-Frequency Words

A. Look at the picture. Then complete each sentence with a word from the box.

> alphabet   heart   mind

1. I learned the letters of the

   _____ last year.

2. I would sing a song about them in

   my _____ .

3. Now I know them all by _____ .

B. Challenge Write a sentence. Use the word *mind*. Then write another sentence using the word *alphabet*.

_____

_____

_____

Words with Long *i*
(*igh* and *ie*)

A. Look at the pictures. Then complete each sentence with a word from the box.

pie	lightning	knight
cried	tie	fright

1. The _____ fills the dark sky with light.

2. The baby _____ for his mother.

3. The _____ wears a hard coat.

4. The _____ was made with apples.

5. The spider in our tent gave us a _____.

6. He wears a _____ around his neck.

B. Challenge Use words from the box to write two sentences about something scary.

_____

_____

_____

Summarize

A. Think about *The First Art Class.* **Finish each sentence so it tells about the story.**

1. The students are waiting for their first _____ class.

gym

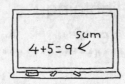
math

art

2. Stan hopes they will use brushes and _____ to make a picture.

markers

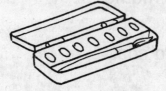
paint

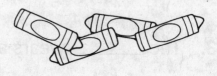
crayons

3. Mr. Hanson has them make and then show _____ art.

clay

crayons

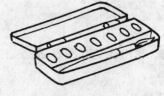
paint

B. Challenge Why do you think Raymond had so much fun working with clay?

_____

_____

_____

Writing

A. Finish the sentences to write a paragraph that summarizes a student's favorite class. Use words and phrases from the word bank.

> art   paint pictures   wall   brushes   red

My favorite class is _____.

I like to _____ with my _____.

I always use the color _____ because it is so bright and bold.

When I am finished, I hang my painting on the _____.

B. Challenge If you were a painter, what would you choose to paint? Finish the paragraph with your answer.

If I were a painter, I would paint _____

_____

_____

_____

Name _____

Vocabulary

A. Choose the BEST sentence to match the picture.
Write A or B on the line.

break

(A) Did you *break* the glass?
(B) I took a *break* from my homework.

1. _____

watch

(A) I like to *watch* the game.
(B) My *watch* tells time.

2. _____

tire

(A) The car *tire* is round.
(B) I *tire* easily and need to rest.

3. _____

shape

(A) The *shape* is a square.
(B) *Shape* the clay with your hand.

4. _____

B. Challenge Use the word *right* in a sentence. Then explain the meaning of the word.

_____

_____

_____

High-Frequency Words

A. Look at the picture. Then complete each sentence with a word from the box.

> below   neighbor   should

1. I look down _____ at the
   moving men.

2. They help my new _____
   move into the house next door.

3. I know I _____ go say hello, but
   I am a little scared.

B. Challenge Write a sentence. Use the word *should*. Then
write another sentence using the word *below*.

_____

_____

_____

_____

Words Ending with *-ed*

A. Look at the pictures. Then complete each sentence with a word from the box.

raked	roped	excited
fished		voted

 **1.** We were _____ because our team won.

 2. The boy _____ the leaves.

 **3.** The swing was _____ around the tree branch.

 4. Tom _____ in the lake.

 **5.** The boys and girls _____ for the best book.

B. Challenge Use words from the box to write a sentence about something you did with a friend.

_____

_____

_____

Summarize and Retell

A. Think about *A Good Idea.* **Finish each sentence so that it tells about the story.**

1. James and Morgan need a safe place to _____.

ride bikes

jump rope

play ball

2. They have an idea to clean up a nearby _____.

lot

park

building

3. Mrs. Taylor paints a mural on _____.

a bench

a wall

an easel

B. Challenge **Why do you think everyone thought that James and Morgan's idea was a good one?**

_____

_____

Name _____

Writing

A. Finish the sentences to write a paragraph that compares and contrasts different sports. Use words and phrases from the word bank.

team	baseball	swimming
bat	hit the ball	tennis

My favorite sport is _____.

I like to _____ with my _____.

Because you hit the ball, it is something like _____.

It is nothing like _____.

I like this sport because you play with a _____.

B. Challenge Compare and contrast your two favorite books. Finish the paragraph with your answer.

My two favorite books are _____ and

_____. They are alike because _____.

They are different because _____.

Vocabulary

A. Circle the BEST meaning based on context clues.

1. Morgan catches the ball in her *mitt.* What does the word *mitt* mean?

(A) glove

(B) mitten

2. They went to the next building to ask a *neighbor* for help.

What does the word *neighbor* mean?

(A) person next door

(B) horse

3. Mrs. Sanchez's class was full of *pride* about the school mural.

What does the word *pride* mean?

(A) good feelings

(B) a lion's family

B. Challenge Read the sentence. Then use context clues to define the word *giant* on a separate sheet of paper.

The neighbors were shocked when they looked out their windows and saw a *giant* picture on the house next door!

High-Frequency Words

A. Look at the pictures. Then label each picture with a word from the box.

> took   should   woman   light

1. The _____ smiles.

2. He _____ a picture

of me.

3. You _____ brush

your teeth after each meal.

4. The _____ lets

Allen read at night.

B. Challenge Use the words *woman* and *light* to write about the picture.

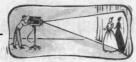

_____

_____

_____

Name _____

Plays

A. Read about the parts of a play. Then answer the question that follows.

Parts of a Play

A good play must have four key parts. First, the play should have a plot. A plot tells what happens. Second, a play needs a setting. The setting of a play describes where the story takes place. Third, a play must have characters. Actors take the parts of characters in a play. Fourth, a play has dialogue. Dialogue is how the characters talk to each other. Use these four parts and your play should be a good one!

How do you think the author feels about plays?

_____

_____

B. Help write a play about magic glasses. Finish the dialogue between the characters in the picture.

Angela: Jose, these glasses must be magic! They are making me feel _____

_____

Jose: Yes! I can see myself in the future! I am

_____

_____

★ READERS' THEATER ★

Let's Put On a Show!

Characters						
Narrator	Abby	Maya	Rao	Jacob	Jesse	Tara

NARRATOR: One afternoon in late summer the kids were sitting on the steps in front of Tara's house.

RAO: What do you want to do now?

MAYA: Let's have a picnic.

TARA: We did that yesterday.

RAO: I don't mind doing it again.

JESSE: Let's do something else.

ABBY: I know! Let's put on a show!

MAYA: A show?

RAO: What kind of show?

ABBY: A talent show! I sing really well!

MAYA: Me, too. I know lots of songs by heart.

ABBY: But I'm the star. The show was my idea.

MAYA: Well, you can't be the only one in the show!

RAO: Let's not argue about it. The show's a good idea.

JESSE: I know—let's do a show for the Fourth of July. We can sing patriotic songs like "Yankee Doodle."

JACOB: I'm good at dancing!

TARA: What about the rest of us? I'm not a good singer.

RAO: I can't do anything either. But we'll need someone to sell tickets.

TARA: I can do that.

JESSE: Do we need scenery? I can paint it. I'm a pretty good artist.

RAO: Okay, it's a plan. We'd better get busy. It's only two weeks until showtime!

END PART 1

PART 2

NARRATOR: Later that week the kids got together again to practice and plan.

ABBY: [*singing*] "Tomorrow! Tomorrow! Tomorrow!"

JESSE: Hey, wait a minute, Abby. That's not a patriotic song. I thought we were doing songs like "Yankee Doodle"?

ABBY: But I like this song. It's my favorite.

JESSE: It's a silly song!

ABBY: Well, I want to sing it!

RAO: How about singing "God Bless America?" Your voice is just right for that!

ABBY: Well, okay.

MAYA: I'm going to sing "It's a Grand Old Flag" but I need to practice it some more. I'm not ready yet.

JACOB: No, you can't. I was going to tap dance to that!

RAO: I know! Maya could sing it twice, and you could tap dance to it the second time.

MAYA: Okay, that will be fun.

JESSE: I have the scenery almost done. Look!

JACOB: Wow, what a beautiful flag you painted.

JESSE: Thanks.

TARA:	How do we end the show?
RAO:	I know. The group can sing something together. Abby and Maya could start. Then Jesse and Jacob could march in and sing with them. Then Jacob and Tara could tap dance while everyone sings and waves little flags.
JESSE:	Rao, that's a terrific idea.
RAO:	Yeah, I guess.
JACOB:	What's wrong, Rao? Why do you look so unhappy?
RAO:	I can't write or sing or dance or paint like all of you can. I can't do anything!
ABBY:	You have really good ideas. Best of all, you got us to work together and stop fighting.
JACOB:	I think your talent is leadership, Rao.
RAO:	Gee, I never thought of that! Thanks!
ABBY:	You know, I think this is going to be a terrific show!

Verbs

A. Choose the BEST answer for each question.

1. Which word is a verb?

| Let's put on a show! |

Ⓐ Let's

Ⓑ put

Ⓒ on

2. Which sentence has an irregular verb?

Ⓐ Wow, what a beautiful flag you painted!

Ⓑ Jacob danced to "Yankee Doodle."

Ⓒ You had really good ideas.

3. Which sentence has the correct singular form of the verb _to be?_

Ⓐ The show is my idea.

Ⓑ The show am my idea.

Ⓒ The show are my idea.

B. Look at the picture. Write a sentence about the kids in the talent show. Use an irregular verb, such as _to go, to have,_ or _to be._

_____

_____

Word Bank

Word	Draw or Write	★ I don't know well. ★★ I understand a little. ★★★ I understand well.

Directions: Have students add words and word meanings. Have them add stars in the third column as they know more about each word.

Name _____

Word Bank

Word	Draw or Write	★ I don't know well. ★★ I understand a little. ★★★ I understand well.

Directions: Have students add words and word meanings. Have them add stars in the third column as they know more about each word.

Name _____

Word Bank

Word	Draw or Write	★ I don't know well. ★★ I understand a little. ★★★ I understand well.

Directions: Have students add words and word meanings. Have them add stars in the third column as they know more about each word.

Word Bank

Word	Draw or Write	★ I don't know well. ★★ I understand a little. ★★★ I understand well.

Directions: Have students add words and word meanings. Have them add stars in the third column as they know more about each word.

Word Bank

Word	Draw or Write	★ I don't know well. ★★ I understand a little. ★★★ I understand well.

Directions: Have students add words and word meanings. Have them add stars in the third column as they know more about each word.

Word Bank

Word	Draw or Write	★ I don't know well. ★★ I understand a little. ★★★ I understand well.

Directions: Have students add words and word meanings. Have them add stars in the third column as they know more about each word.

Word Bank

Word	Draw or Write	★ I don't know well. ★★ I understand a little. ★★★ I understand well.

Directions: Have students add words and word meanings. Have them add stars in the third column as they know more about each word.

Word Bank

Word	Draw or Write	★ I don't know well. ★★ I understand a little. ★★★ I understand well.

Directions: Have students add words and word meanings. Have them add stars in the third column as they know more about each word.

Name _____

Word Bank

Word	Draw or Write	★ I don't know well. ★★ I understand a little. ★★★ I understand well.

Directions: Have students add words and word meanings. Have them add stars in the third column as they know more about each word.

Word Bank

Word	Draw or Write	★ I don't know well. ★★ I understand a little. ★★★ I understand well.

Directions: Have students add words and word meanings. Have them add stars in the third column as they know more about each word.

Name _____

Word Bank

Word	Draw or Write	★ I don't know well. ★★ I understand a little. ★★★ I understand well.

Directions: Have students add words and word meanings. Have them add stars in the third column as they know more about each word.

Name _____

Word Bank

Word	Draw or Write	★ I don't know well. ★★ I understand a little. ★★★ I understand well.

Directions: Have students add words and word meanings. Have them add stars in the third column as they know more about each word.

Word Bank

Word	Draw or Write	★ I don't know well. ★★ I understand a little. ★★★ I understand well.

Directions: Have students add words and word meanings. Have them add stars in the third column as they know more about each word.

Name _____

Word Bank

Word	Draw or Write	★ I don't know well. ★★ I understand a little. ★★★ I understand well.

Directions: Have students add words and word meanings. Have them add stars in the third column as they know more about each word.